Artificial Neural Networks,
Dynamical Systems
and Self-Organization

RITA PIZZI

MARIALESSIA MUSUMECI

CONTENTS

1

INTRODUCTION

A. Self-organization, complex systems and chaos

The theory of complex systems aims to analyze and forecast their behavior of the interaction between many elementary components [1], using mathematical and other formal tools. It also studies self-organization, i.e. the organization that emerges spontaneously from complex systems that, in presence of suitable conditions, react to external environment changes reorganizing themselves so to exhibit novel properties [2][3].

A classic example is a fluid heated from the bottom. In the presence of appropriate boundary conditions, the convective motions of the molecules are arranged according to the so-called Bénard columns, that are vertical honeycomb formations. This unexpected cooperation between molecules is established whereas the system would simply be expected to increase in molecular disorder. The system reacted to the external environment modifications by reorganizing in such a way as to exhibit an innovative property [3].

Self-organization can be defined a space-time structure that is not imposed from outside but emerges spontaneously from the evolution of the system as a function of its dynamics. The emerging organization is observable at a different space-time scale, much greater than the molecular one.

The development of mathematical models for such systems [4] shows that the equations that hold them are generally extremely sensitive to the initial conditions, so that extremely small fluctuations give rise to completely different dynamical stories (the famous Lorentz's "butterfly effect" [5]). This indeterminacy in real terms (but not in principle) is not avoidable, since for any numerical system a not infinite degree of precision must be fixed, and any degree, even the highest possible, will produce different dynamical stories. This represents the so-called "deterministic chaos": the system has a behavior altogether regular but irregular in detail, thus it is impossible to predict its future behavior.

We define *chaos* the unpredictable behavior of deterministic dynamical systems because of their sensitivity to initial conditions [6]. The behavior of a deterministic dynamical system is predictable once the initial conditions are known. But there are cases in which depending on the precision with which we measure the initial conditions, the motion of the system behaves very differently. More precisely, a set S exhibits sensitivity to the initial values if there is a neighborhood ρ such as for each $\varepsilon > 0$ and for every x in S, there exists a y such that

$$|x - y| < \varepsilon \quad \text{and} \quad |x_n - y_n| > \rho \quad \text{for some} \quad n > 0.$$

Then there exists a fixed distance ρ such that, no matter how precisely an initial state is specified, there are neighboring states that eventually move away more than the distance ρ. This is what happens in chaotic systems.

A typical example of self-organization is present in all biological systems [7] and in their more evolved expression, intelligent life.

Also computational models are becoming more and more advanced, being able to simulate quite complex real systems. A promising attempt to reproduce advanced functionalities by means of the collective behavior of simple elements is given, as specified below, by the Artificial Neural Networks paradigm: multiple interconnected elements exchange information on the basis of a series of input from the outside, and realize a form of functional organization that is not directly derivable from the algorithm imposed from the outside, but emerges from the complexity of the system.

B. Complexity and non-Linearity

In the traditional approach the complex systems are processed analytically, i.e. are reduced to a linear combination of elements. A classic linear relationship is the Hook's law ($F=-kx$, where x is the spring length and F the applied force) which regulates the elastic force. But when the elasticity is lost (e.g. straining the spring or the rubber band too much) the graph ceases to be linear. The system is not linear anymore, and in specific conditions it shows a sudden change of behavior: the rubber band breaks.

In nature many systems are linear or approximated to linearity (e.g. the electromagnetic wave equations), and this allowed the modeling of many natural phenomena. But for many physical systems linearity is not sustainable, and their modeling becomes extremely complex: as we will see in the following, almost all dynamical systems exhibit a chaotic behavior, i.e. they are not inherently nondeterministic, but in fact unpredictable [8][9].

The processing of strongly time-varying and not strictly linear space-time patterns, such as those coming from the acquisition of real-world data, is an issue of growing importance, and its complexity involves necessarily the use and development of advanced mathematical tools.

The typical adaptivity of the Artificial Neural Networks and their generalization ability seems to indicate them as a valid choice for the analysis of these systems. We will examine them in more detail in the following.

C. Non-Linearity and Dynamical Systems

We call linear the functions which behave in such a way that

$$f(ax+by) = af(x)+bf(y)$$

where this equality is not held, the function is called non-linear, and everything becomes mathematically more difficult.

For example if

$$f(x) = 0 \quad \text{and} \quad f(y) = 0$$

$f(ax + by)$ is no more equal to zero for any a and b (superposition principle: more solutions exist for each variable) and the solution must be sought with special methods.

A function that models real world is hardly linear, but is often approximated to a linear function. Non-linear systems exhibit complex effects that are not deducible with linear methods. This is particularly evident for dynamical systems [10] [11].

A system is called *dynamical system* when it expresses the variability of a state X (or a point in a vector space) in time:

$$\frac{dX}{dt} = F(x,t) \quad F : W \subset R^n \to R^n \quad \text{differentiable} \qquad (1)$$

The solution of the system is the set of trajectories as a function of the initial conditions. A dynamical system is completely defined by a *phase space* or *state space*, whose coordinates describe him at all times, and by a rule that specifies the future trend of all the state variables.

Dynamical systems are said deterministic if there is only one solution for each state, stochastic if there are several solutions following a certain probability distribution (e.g. the toss of a coin).

The phase space is the collection of all possible states of a dynamical system. It can be finite (as in the case of the coin, two states) or infinite (if the variables are real numbers).

For example, a cellular automaton is a dynamical system with discrete time, discrete geometric space and discrete state space $s(i, j)$, where i are the spatial coordinates, j is the time, and the update rule is

$$s(i, j + 1) = f(s) .$$

A simple example is the case of the pendulum, in which the phase space is continuous, two-dimensional and its coordinates are angle and speed.

If we include time as a coordinate of the phase space we represent the dynamical system with the above mentioned differential equation (1),

where (X, t) is the phase space.

Mathematically, a dynamical system is described by an initial value problem. The trajectory in the phase space traced by a solution of an initial value problem is called *trajectory* of the dynamical system.

We define constant trajectory a constant solution

$$x(t) = x(0)$$

of (1), i.e. a vector $x(0)$ for which each component of the right side of (1) is zero.

A constant trajectory is said *stable* if the following conditions are met:

a) there must be a positive number ε such that each trajectory beginning within ε of $x(0)$ must asymptotically approach $x(0)$

b) for each positive number ε a positive number $\delta(\varepsilon)$ must exist such that a trajectory is guaranteed to stay within ε of $x(0)$ simply requiring it to start within $\delta(\varepsilon)$ of $x(0)$.

c) the set of all points that can be initial states of trajectories that asymptotically approach a stable trajectory is said *region of attraction* of the stable trajectory.

A *limit cycle*, or *cyclic attractor*, is a closed curve in the n-dimensional space with the following properties:

a) no constant trajectory is contained in the limit cycle

b) any trajectory that begins in a point of the limit cycle must lie within the limit cycle also later on

c) for each positive number ε there must be a positive number $\delta(\varepsilon)$ such that a trajectory is guaranteed to stay within ε of the limit cycle simply requiring it to begin within $\delta(\varepsilon)$ of the limit cycle.

In summary, if some trajectories converge in some point, the set of initial states of these generated trajectories is said *region of attraction* of the point. A region of attraction is ultimately a set of points in the state space delimiting a finite diameter region such that each trajectory enters and never gets out.

1 NON-LINEAR ANALYTICAL METHODS

A very common type of self-organization, which in nature is established also outside the life phenomena (e.g. involving meteorological and astronomical phenomena, fluid dynamics, etc.), as mentioned above, is the deterministic chaos. The long-term behavior of the chaotic systems follows structured patterns detectable by displaying the system trajectories in the state space. These trajectories exhibit a spatial structure in which they are confined in a strange attractor (i.e. they exhibit some regularity but never repeat themselves exactly) [12]. A strange attractor is geometrically a fractal [13], i.e. a structure with a non-integer dimension.

A. Fractal Dimension and Correlation Dimension

Define dimension D of an object the exponent which connects its extent b with the linear distance r :

$$b \propto r^{D}$$

The extent b can refer to the linear distance, area, volume, or the amount of information in bits.

For a line $b \propto r^1$ (and in fact a line has dimension 1), for a plan $b \propto r^2$, etc. Taking the logarithms we obtain

$$D = \lim_{r \to 0} \frac{\log b}{\log r}$$

It is possible to have non-integer dimension objects, the so-called *fractals* [13], [14]. They have the important feature to be self-similar, i.e. they do not possess a characteristic scale. For example a branch is a fractal object of dimension between 1 and 2.

It is shown that chaotic attractors have a fractal (or Hausdorff) dimension > 2.

It has been shown for example that the fractal dimension of eyes-closed EEG (about 2) is lower than the open-eyes EEG dimension (about 6). As we will see in detail below, according to W. Freeman [15], [16], [17] a chaotic brain activity prepares for the perception of a particular stimulus, and its trajectories end up within a periodic (limit cycle) or chaotic basin of attraction.

Even time series may exhibit characteristics of stochasticity or chaotic organization [18].

To assess the dimension of a series a procedure called *delay-time embedding* is used. If a time series is long enough, the trajectory of the state space generated by it is geometrically equivalent to the attractor of the system that generated the original series.

Grassberger and Procaccia [19] have developed a method, often applied to physiological data, which allows to determine the so-called *D2 correlation dimension* (which corresponds to a lower limit for the fractal dimension).

We replace each observation in the original signal $X(t)$ with the vector:

$$y(i) = x(i), x(i+d), x(i+2d), ..., x(i+(m-1)d)$$

obtaining as a result a series of vectors of m coordinates in an m-dimensional space:

$$Y = y(1), y(2), ..., y(N-(m-1)d))$$

where N is the length of the original series and d the so-called *lag* or *delay time*, i.e. the number of points between the components of each reconstructed state vector.

It can be shown that the reconstructed state vectors are topologically invariant transformations of the original state vectors, and that the set of state vectors (points in the m-dimensional space) formed by Y in the reconstructed space has the same dimension of the attractor of the system.

It also demonstrates (Taken's Theorem) that there is a mathematical relationship between the embedding dimension n of the series and the dimension of the attractor of the corresponding dynamical system:

$$n = 2d + 1.$$

Now, the dimension $D2$ is defined as

$$D2 = \lim_{r \to 0} \frac{\log C(r)}{\log r}$$

where the extension of the series is given by the *correlation integral* $C(r)$.

The correlation integral is calculated as the average number of state vectors that stay within a distance r from each other. In other words, $C(r)$ calculates the average number of points that are on the corresponding reconstructed attractor. If the attractor is a fractal, for a certain range of r (the range in which fractals are perfectly self-similar) the logarithm of this average will have a linear relationship with the logarithm of r.

In this region the slope of the curve measures the *correlation dimension D2*. The correlation dimension $D2$ gives the measure of the complexity of the system attractor and, in the way shown above, is connected to the correlation integral, which instead measures the extension of the attractor.

The graph of the correlation dimension is expressed as a function of the embedding dimension. Ideally, the graph should converge asymptotically to the real correlation dimension.

In a time series the concept of self-similarity is used in a distributional sense: if viewed at a different scale, the object distribution remains unchanged. In such a case a long-range dependency occurs, i.e. the values at each instant are correlated to the values of all the successive instants.

A self-similar time series has the property that when aggregated into a shorter series (where each point is the sum of multiple original points) it maintains the same autocorrelation function

$$r(k) = E[(X_t - \mu)(X_{t+k} - \mu)]$$

both in the series $X = (X_t : t = 0,1,2, ...)$ and in the contracted series $X^{(m)} = (X_k^{(m)} : k = 1,2,3, ...)$, aggregated in blocks of size m. So the series is distributionally self-similar, because the distribution of the aggregate series is the same (except for a scale variation) as the original. As a result, the self-similar processes show long-range dependency, i.e. have an autocorrelation function

$$r(k) \sim k - \beta \text{ for } k \to \infty, \qquad 0 < \beta < 1$$

i.e. the function decays hyperbolically.

B. *Hurst Parameter*

The degree of self-similarity of a series is expressible using a single parameter [20], that indicates the rate of decay of the autocorrelation function and is said *Hurst parameter H* :

$$H = 1 - \beta / 2$$

So for a self-similar series

$$\tfrac{1}{2} < H < 1.$$

For H tending to 1 the amount of self-similarity increases, thus the series is self-similar when it departs significantly from ½. It is shown that the Hurst parameter is linked to the Hausdorff fractal dimension D (of which the correlation dimension $C(r)$ is the lower limit) from the simple expression

$$D = 2 - H.$$

For example the jagged coast lines, which have $D \approx 1.2$, lead to a value of H equal to 0.8.

C. Recurrent Plots

A qualitative assessment method of an expanded series with time-delay embedding are the *Recurrent Plots*, representing a matrix based on the Euclidean distances of the embedded series. The recurrent plots can be displayed with a color code, and the more structured they are, the more the system moves away from the stochasticity [21].

The *Recurrence Quantification Analysis* (RQA) is a new quantitative tool that can be applied to the analysis of Recurrent plots of a time series reconstructed with a delay-time embedding method.

The RQA is independent from the data dimension, from stationarity and from assumptions about the statistical data distribution. RQA provides a local view of the behavior of the series, because it analyzes the distances of pairs of points, and not a distribution of distances. Therefore unlike autocorrelation, RQA is capable to analyze fast transients and locate in time the characteristics of a dynamical variation: for this reason RQA is the ideal tool for the analysis of physiological systems.

There are different quantifiers for the evaluation of recurrent plots: the most significant is DET (Determinism), i.e. the percentage of recurring points that appear in sequence forming diagonal lines in the matrix. DET gives the measure of the space portions in which the system holds for a longer time than expected by pure chance.

The observation of recurrent points consecutive in time (that form lines parallel to the main diagonal) is an important sign of deterministic structure. In fact, the length of the longest (recurrent) diagonal line in the recurrent plot predicts accurately the value of the maximum Lyapounov exponent of the series.

The Lyapounov exponent is another measure of the determinism of a series, which quantifies the average speed of divergence of nearby trajectories along various directions of the phase space.

Given a derivable function T and a dynamical system created by its iteration, the derivative of T at the point x_0 gives the velocity with which the points close to x_0 move away after one iteration.

We define a Lyaponov exponent of the point x_0, namely of the orbit $(x_0, x_1, x_2, ..., x_n)$, the limit (if existing)

$$\lambda(x_0) = \lim_{n \to \infty}(\log | \frac{dT^n(x_0)}{dx} |)$$

of the logarithm of the velocity with which the points close to x_0 moved away after n iterations. Thus after a very long time the distance between two orbits near to x_0 has grown with a factor approximatively equal to $e^{\lambda(x_0)n}$, that quantifies the speed of their divergence.

It is shown that chaotic systems have a positive maximum Lyapounov exponent.

2   Artificial Neural Networks

as Dynamical Systems

A. Stability and Region of Attraction in Neural Models

An Artificial Neural Network (ANN) can be seen as a dynamical system which gives account for the dynamics of n neurons.

Each neuron is mathematically defined by its state $x(i)$ and its function $g = g(x_i)$ (gain) differentiable everywhere and nondecrescent. A typical gain function is the logistic function

$$g(x) = \left(1 + e^{-x}\right)^{-1}$$

biologically motivated because it simulates the refractory phase of natural neurons. This feature provides values between 0 and 1. But it is often useful to use a transfer function symmetrical with respect to zero, so to keep any symmetry of the input values. Thus the hyperbolic tangent function (values between -1 and +1) is used, or the function

$$F(P) = \frac{A\left(e^{kp} - 1\right)}{\left(e^{kp} + 1\right)}$$

with positive constants A and k.

The rate of change of each x_i is determined by a function dependent on x_i and on the outputs $g_i(x_i)$. In general we can express this change with the system of differential equations

$$\frac{dx_i}{dt} = -k_i x_i + p_i(g(x)) \qquad (2)$$

where k_i is a positive constant, and each p_i is an in general polynomial function of n variables $g_1(x(t))$, $g_2(x(t))$, ..., $g_n(x(t))$, which behave well enough to make sure that the trajectories for the system of equations exist and are unique.

By trajectory we mean a series of points in an n-dimensional space that depart from some initial state (at time zero) in the n-space to a final state. The task of the Artificial Neural Network is to generate such a set of points up to the final state, which constitutes the output of the network.

The levels of activity of n neurons are represented by a point in the n-dimensional space [22]. Therefore we build an n-dimensional dynamical system whose solutions are trajectories representing constant attractors (stable equilibrium) or cyclic attractors (limit cycles).

We say that *the purpose of the Artificial Neural Network is to generate trajectories in the n-dimensional space that are asymptotically approaching some of the constant attractor trajectories.*

In the additive neural models (as the Multilayer Perceptron, see below) each p_i is a linear function of the components of g:

$$p_i = \sum_j^n T_{ij} g_i \qquad (3)$$

where T_{ij} are real constants forming an $n \times n$ matrix.

However, recently higher order Artificial Neural Networks have emerged as more efficient. In this kind of networks, each p_i is a polynomial function of the components of g : typically of the form

$$g_1^{e_1} g_2^{e_2} \cdots g_n^{e_n}$$

where each exponent e_i is 0 or 1.

For linear networks of the type (3) the Cohen - Grossberg theorem [23] ensures the existence of stable points (i.e. points such that $\frac{dx(P)}{dt} = 0$).

Cohen-Grossberg THEOREM:

Every dynamical system of the form

$$\frac{dx_i}{dt} = a_i(x_i)[b_i(x_i) - \sum_j W_{ij} S_{ij}(x_j)]$$

s.t.

1) The matrix w_{ij} is symmetrical and each $w_{ij} \geq 0$

2) The function $a_j(x)$ is continuous for $x \geq 0$ and $a_j(x) > 0$ for $x > 0$

3) The function $b_j(x)$ is continuous and does not tend to infinity for any open interval for $x > 0$

4) The function $S_{ij}(x)$ is differentiable and $S_{ij}'(x) > 0$ for $x \geq 0$

5) $b_i(x) - W_i S_i < 0$ for $x \to \infty$

has an at least countable set of stable points P such that $\dfrac{dx(P)}{dt} = 0$.

If the network status at time 0 is such that $x_i(0) > 0$, then the ANN will converge usually at some stable point P (i.e. such that $\dfrac{dx(P)}{dt} = 0$), and at least a countable set of such points will exist.

Although these conditions are restrictive, they match those supported by many hetero- and autoassociative ANNs (see below the Hopfield network, with fully interconnected nodes and symmetrical weights). The memories are set in the attractors, and the theorem guarantees their existence, although there are many spurious attractors (Fig.1).

To any state of a network an energy Lyapounov function can be associated that allows you to determine certain properties of the trajectories. A Lyapounov function L is a function

$$L : \{0,1\}^n \to R \ , \quad L(T(x)) \leq L(x)$$

for each $x \in \{0,1\}^n$, where T is the transition function operated by the network.

Thus L is monotone non-increasing along each trajectory. It follows that the equilibrium points of the system correspond to the minimum points of L. For networks with a square connection matrix, the L function is called energy function and is chosen as

$$E(x) = -\frac{1}{2}\sum_i \sum_j w_{ij} x_i x_j$$

where one can easily see that it is monotone non-increasing and $\Delta E \leq 0$ anytime , i.e. the system is globally stable.

This is the case for the Hopfield network [24], an obvious example of how an ANN is a dynamical system that can tend to a series of stable attractors.

It is a fully connected network with symmetrical weights, with bipolar input $(+/- 1$ or $0/1)$. The inputs are applied to all nodes simultaneously, and the weights are set according to the law

$$w_{ij} = \sum x_i x_j \quad \text{for } i \neq j$$
$$w_{ij} = 0 \quad \text{for } i = j$$

In the learning cycle each output of a neuron is a new input for the same neuron. The calculation of the new value is established by the function

$$f(x_i) = x_i \qquad \text{if} \quad \sum w_{ij} x_j = T_i$$

(threshold possibly equal to zero)

$$f(x_i) = +1 \qquad \text{if} \quad \sum w_{ij} x_j > T_i$$

$$f(x_i) = -1 \qquad \text{if} \quad \sum w_{ij} x_j < T_i$$

We can see an input pattern as a point in the state space that, while the network iterates, moves gradually toward minima, which represent stable states of the network. The last values of the weights represent the output of the network. The solution occurs when the point moves to the lowest region of the basin of attraction. In fact, as for symmetric matrices with diagonal equal to zero

$$\frac{\Delta E}{\Delta x_i} = -\sum w_{ij} x_j$$

$$\text{if } \Delta x_i < 0 \qquad \sum w_{ij} x_j < 0$$

$$\text{if } \Delta x_i > 0 \qquad \sum w_{ij} x_j > 0$$

i.e. always $\Delta E \leq 0$.

After a number of iterations the network will stabilize in a state of minimum energy. Each minimum corresponds to a pattern stored in the network. An unknown pattern constitutes a point on this hyperplane, which gradually moves toward a minimum. There may be so-called metastable states, i.e. minimum points that don't have a corresponding stored pattern (spurious attractors).

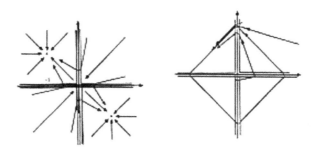

Fig. 1 - Typical trajectories in a two dimensional space
with two memories and a limit cycle model

More generally the following theorem holds:

THEOREM: (4)

Each ANN model of type (2) has a finite region of attraction.

B. *Learning*

Once a particular dynamical model and its attractors have been identified, a learning algorithm is to be established that varies the locations of fixed points to encode information. Therefore a condition sufficient for the existence of such an algorithm is the existence of isolated stable attractors in the system, i.e. of fixed points.

The weight matrix is to be adjusted in such a way as, given an initial state $x_0=x(t_0)$, a fixed point $x_\infty=x(t_\infty)$ corresponds to a given input, and the fixed point has components that have a desired set of values D_i in the output units.

A typical method, used in the backpropagation networks, is to minimize a function E that measures the distance between the desired fixed point (attractor) and the current fixed point:

$$E = \frac{1}{2}\sum_i J_i^2$$

where

$$J_i = (D_i - x_{i\infty})Q_i$$

and Q_i is a function whose value is 1 or 0 according to whether the i-th unit belongs or not to the output subset of the network units. Then the learning algorithm will move the fixed points so as to satisfy on the output units the equation

$$x(t_\infty) = D_i$$

A typical way to do this is to let the system evolve in the weight space along the trajectories antiparallel to the gradient of E:

$$\tau\frac{dw_{ij}}{dt} = -\frac{dE}{dw_{ij}}$$

Where τ is a numeric constant that defines the temporal scale with which the weights are changing. τ must be small, so that x could always be substantially constant, i.e. $x(t_\infty) = x_\infty$.

When on the output layer the error is computed between current output and desired output, this is propagated backwards to the other layers, in such a way as to adjust weights of any single node.

This algorithm, that is called gradient descent, is used by the backpropagation networks [25]; it is not the only possible algorithm but is no doubt the easiest and most effective equation for the minimization of E.

It can be shown that, if the initial network is stable, the gradient descent dynamics does not change the network stability. This allows to state the reliability of the backpropagation algorithm, that yields the necessary robustness to the deviations generated by the noise present in real systems.

3 NEURAL MODELS OF DYNAMICAL SYSTEMS PROCESSING

A. Spatiotemporal Patterns in Artificial Neural Networks.

ANNs have been initially applied to problems regarding spatial or instantaneous patterns, but the evolution of technology has made it necessary to apply them also to spatiotemporal pattern. By spatiotemporal pattern we mean a function $x(t)$ that associates at any time t a point in the n-dimensional input space:

$$x(t):\{t_0,t_1\} \to R^n$$

In three dimensions, it is possible to represent a spatiotemporal pattern as a trajectory in the input space parameterized as a function of time. The task of the ANN will be to implement a time-variant transformation, that associates an output function $y(t)$ to the function $x(t)$ for each time t.

Several methods have been proposed in the past to allow the

ANNs to process the spatiotemporal patterns, i.e. to generate parameterized attractor trajectories over time. These methods can be classified mainly in the following variants [26]:

- Creation of a spatial representation of temporal data

- Setting of time-delays in neurons or connections

- Use of neurons with activations that add up the inputs over time

- Combinations of the above methods.

The earliest strategy was to convert the output data into a sequence of data. When a new set of inputs is received, the previous data are deleted and so on. The network preserves the memory of the past only in the intermediate layers.

Then the so-called time-delay networks were studied, in which the information at an instant of time is moved to the right in a chain of nodes, while the new information is added to the left. The number of nodes determines the number of time intervals on which information is sampled.

An architecture that leads to stable states without time-delay can produce oscillations or a chaotic behavior (with cyclic or chaotic attractors) once the delay is introduced. Instead, if the delay is transmitted in the connections, the information remains in a certain state for a period, then a connection is triggered that brings it to another state and so on. It can be proved that such networks, which are obviously equipped with long or short-term memory, are able to reproduce different types of temporal sequences.

Another method is to change the neurons in such a way that they are able to add up data that arrive through time, allowing a gradual decay of the older information. If neurons have Recurrent connections, the feedback acts creating hysteresis in each neuron, thus a memory of the information that persists beyond the stimulus.

ANNs have also been proposed that accept input information coded in the form of frequencies, as actually occurs in the natural sensors. These networks were used to drive robotic actuators, with good results in the hardware implementation. The simplest of the above described ANNs are networks not equipped with memory, with static architecture, which does not include any actual management of the time variable [27].

B. Recurrent Neural Networks

The so-called dynamical (in the strict sense) networks have proved to be more efficient in processing time-dependent inputs. Their architecture [28] is characterized by a feedback system called state feedback (Fig. 2), achieved through appropriate connections between the nodes. It consists of the fact that a node receives as afferent signals both the inputs and all the outputs of the other nodes, including its own. An internal state of the network becomes definable, which all the nodes in the network with their current outputs contribute to.

These networks can be described by differential equations of the type

$$\frac{du_i(t)}{dt} = -\frac{u_i(t)}{t_i} + \sum_j w_{ij} g\left(u_j(t)\right) + I_i(t)$$

where $u_i(t)$ is the internal state of the *i-th* unit, t_i is the time constant of the *i-th* unit, w_{ij} are the connection weights, $I_i(t)$ is the input of the *i-th* unit and $g(u_j(t))$ is the output of the *i-th* unit.

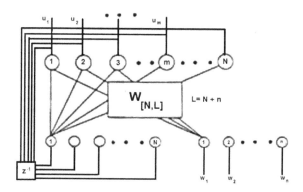

Fig. 2 - Recurrent network with state feedback

Pineda [29] shows that this system of equations is reduced to the system (2) through a simple linear transformation.

Recurrent Neural Networks are ultimately nothing more than networks that possess complex connections between the nodes, in contrast to the feedforward networks which bind the connections to a single direction (from input towards the output) [30].

This model includes a large class of ANNs, from the Hopfield network to the Recurrent backpropagation networks.

As mentioned, Recurrent Neural Networks give better performances than feedforward networks in the treatment of spatiotemporal pattern and in general in the modeling of real dynamical systems. For such systems theorems exist [31][32] showing that time-finite trajectories of a given *n*-dimensional dynamical system are approximated by the internal states of the output units of a Recurrent network with *n* units of output, *N* hidden nodes and appropriate initial states.

In this way the theorem of existence of attractors in the case of Recurrent Neural Networks is guaranteed by the same theorem (4).

The multilayer perceptron (MLP) is suitable to be turned into a Recurrent neural network according to various possible schemes, the more classic of which is due to K. Narendra [33] and is visible in Fig. 3:

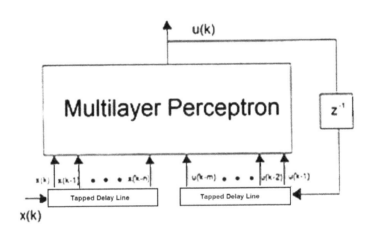

Fig. 3 - Narendra Architecture

The input layer is connected to a tapped delay line, where the sequence of data to be processed is flowing. In another delay line flow the output observations. The only output *u(k)* is function of the *n* input observations and of the *m* previous outputs. The *n+m-ple* of inputs is interpretable as a point in the input space.

Following the method introduced by Rumelhart and Williams and improved by Pineda [34][35][29] the following model is obtained.

The node equation is

$$u_i(k+1) = f\left(\sum_j w_{ij} \, u_j(k)\right) + v_i(k)) \qquad 0 \le k \le n$$

The first layer output is

$$
\begin{aligned}
z_j &= u_j(k) && 0 \le j \le N \\
z_j &= v_j(k) && N+1 \le j \le L
\end{aligned}
$$

where z_j is the output of the first layer and v_j the current input.

The current output is

$$u'_i(k+1) = f\left(I_i(k)\right)$$

where

$$I_i(k) = \sum_j w_{ij} \, z_j(k) + z_0 \qquad (z_0 \; bias)$$

and the node equation is

$$u_i(k+1) = f\left(I_i(k)\right)$$

where f is sigmoid function. The learning algorithm is similar to that of the static MLP. Despite Recurrent Neural Networks are an advanced treatment method for spatiotemporal patterns [30], high variability in the data limits the performance of this ANN model in the use in real time due to the difficulty of finding an exhaustive training set and/or to the length of the learning process [36] [37].

Applications suffer from severe limitations in computational speed or alternately in the ability to adapt to input fluctuations, being difficult to arrive at a positive compromise between the slow online learning process and the poor off-line learning performances. This issue is intrinsic to the supervised learning method.

C. Self-Organizing Networks

An almost forced alternative to the limits of this architecture seems to be constituted by the unsupervised ANNs [38] [39], whose most classical and still effective explication remains currently the Self-Organizing Map (SOM) of T. Kohonen.

The SOM was developed in the 80s by T. Kohonen [40] based on previous studies of neurophysiology. In fact the SOM mechanism was written taking into account the neurophysiological mapping of sensory stimuli on the neocortex, where similar inputs are mapped to nearby locations of the cortex in an orderly and topology-conservative fashion.

The structure of a Kohonen network consists of a layer of N elements, said competitive layer. Each of these receives n signals x_1, ...,x_n that originate from an input layer of n elements, whose connections have weight w_{ij} (Fig.4).

If the competitive layer has a matrix topology, neurons are connected to each other in a square, hexagonal or rhomboid pattern.

If they are vector-based, neurons are simply connected together to form a chain.

To estimate the input intensity I_i of each of the Kohonen layer elements the process is as follows:

$$I_i = D\left(w_i, x\right)$$
$$w_i = \left(w_{i_1}, \ldots, w_{i_n}\right)^T$$
$$x_i = \left(x_1, \ldots, x_n\right)^T$$

where $D(u, x)$ is some distance function, e.g. the Euclidean one.

At this point a competition is put in place to assess which element has the smaller intensity input (i.e .which w_i is the nearest to x). The SOM provides a so-called lateral inhibition mechanism, that is also present in nature in the form of chemical transformations at the synaptic level.

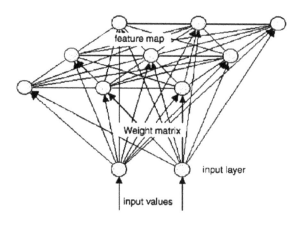

Fig. 4 - Kohonen SOM

In the cortical region of the brain, in fact, neurons physically close to an active neuron show stronger bonds, while at a certain distance from the active neuron inhibitor bonds begin to appear. In this architecture, each element receives both excitatory stimuli from the adjacent elements (the so-called neighborhood), both inhibitors stimuli by the more distant elements, according to the so-called "Mexican-hat" shape (Fig. 5).

The existence of the neighborhood is useful not to polarize the network on a few winning neurons.

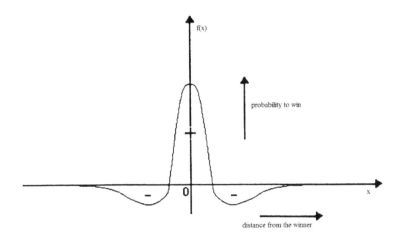

Fig. 5 - Lateral Inhibition

In this way only the elements with distance below a certain value are activated, in restrictive cases only the unit with minimum distance is activated. At this point the learning phase takes place, according to the so-called "Winner Take All" law (WTA).

The training data consist of a sequence of input vectors x. The

Kohonen layer then decides the winner neuron on the basis of the minimum distance. Now the weights are modified according to the law

$$w_{inew} = w_{iold} + \alpha(x - w_{iold})z_i$$

where $0 < \alpha < 1$ slowly decreases over time with the law

$$\alpha(t) = \alpha[1 - t/\delta]$$

where δ is a suitable constant. Being $z_i \neq 0$ only for the winning neuron, the weights of the winning neurons rotate more and more towards the closest vectors, up to ideally overlap with them (Fig. 6).

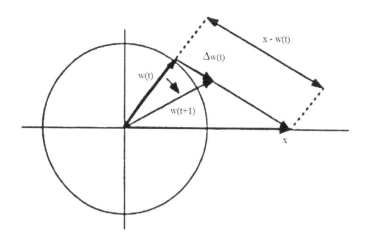

Fig. 6 - Rotation of the weight vectors

In this way the SOM performs a vector quantization, that is a mapping from a space with many dimensions to a space with a smaller number of dimensions, preserving the initial topology.

In other words a Nearest Neighbor (NN) form of clustering is carried out, in which each element of the competitive layer represents the class of the input elements.

The NN method classifies a pattern according to the smallest value obtained among all the distances from a set of reference patterns. This method is useful for separating classes representable by segments of hyperplanes.

For this reason, the SOM classifies correctly pattern topologically well distributed, but shows difficulties in the case of non-linear distributions.

Moreover the importance of the initial weight configuration appears evident, as it must be the most similar to the input topology.

4 PROCESSING DYNAMICAL SYSTEMS IN REAL TIME

A. The ITSOM Architecture

Various are, however, the reasons which in turn limit the SOM performances in the case of strictly non-linear and time-varying input. The first reason is that if the non-linearity of the input topology is too accentuated, the competitive layer is not capable to disentangle itself enough on the form of that topology.

The second reason concerns the difficulty of ensuring convergence (due to the lack of ability to establish a network error for each epoch). The third reason is the low output cardinality, limited to number of competitive layer neurons.

Another problem of the SOM, typical of any clustering algorithm, and the lack of output explication. Once the classification output is obtained, the user must extrapolate the significance with an ad-hoc procedure, which in real-time applications can further penalize the computational load.

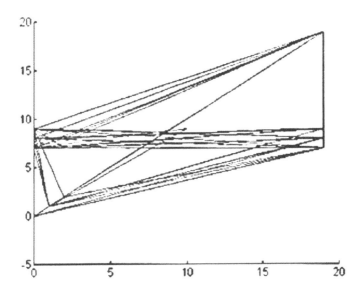

Fig. 7- Series of the winning neurons in 2-dimensional state space
x axis and y axis indicate the weight order values

A proven successful solution was found observing the time series the SOM winning neurons epoch after epoch (Fig. 7). It can be shown in fact that this series forms attractors that hold through epochs and that identify univocally the input pattern that generated them.

On the basis of this evidence the ITSOM (Inductive Tracing Self-Organizing Map) model was developed, whose architecture is described below.

The time sequence of the SOM winning neurons tends to repeat creating chaotic attractors or precise limit cycles that uniquely characterize the input that produced them: in fact, the learning rule implies that the winning weight represents an approximation of the input. At every epoch the new winning weight, along with the weight that won in the previous epoch, constitutes a second order approximation of the input value, and so on.

So it is possible to derive the input value by comparing the characteristic configurations of each input with a set of reference configurations, whose value is known.

In this way a real process of induction is realized, because once a vector quantization many-to-few from the input layer on the weight layer is carried out, a few-to-many step is operated from reference configurations to the whole input (Fig. 8).

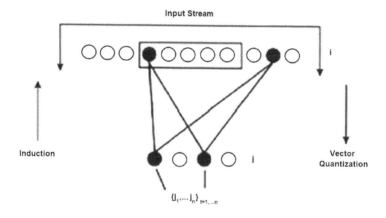

Fig. 8 - ITSOM Architecture

This form of induction is much finer than that obtainable from the only final winning neurons of the a SOM network, because the choice among a set of competitive layer neurons is too limited to provide a meaningful classification. Instead the possible ITSOM outputs are 2^n, where n is the number of neurons of the competitive layer, that make it possible to finely discriminate the input features.

It should be emphasized that the ITSOM does not need to be brought to convergence, because the winning neurons configurations reach the necessary stability within a few tens of epochs.

It was verified that for best results the network should not polarize on too few neurons but even not disperse throughout the layer.

The best suited algorithm to recognize the configurations created by the network is based on the z-score method.

The cumulative scores for each input are normalized according to the distribution of the standardized variable z given by

$$z = \frac{(x - \mu)}{\sigma}$$

where μ is the average of the scores on the neurons of the competitive layer and σ is the standard deviation.

Once set a threshold $0 < \tau \leq 1$, which therefore constitutes one of the parameters of this type of network, we put

$$z = 1 \quad for\ z > \tau$$
$$z = 0 \quad for\ z \leq \tau$$

In this way, each configuration of winning neurons is represented by a binary number formed by as many ones and zeros as many the output layer neurons.

Then it is immediate to use these binary numbers as templates of the input patterns.

Both SOM and other ANNs base their learning process on the cyclic repetition of the input stimulus. Even in the brain there is evidence of reverberating circuits that strengthen the input information on the cortical map.

However it seems unlikely that these loops can be repeated thousands of times in search of a fixed target, also because it is difficult to support the hypothesis that the brain recognizes the last activated neuron as the only information carrier.

It appears more reasonable that the reverberation activities run out spontaneously with the exhaustion of the electrical firing process, and that the cortical maps is formed by a constellation of activated neurons, the so-called mnestic traces, which in the following will be used to recover information.

For this reason the ITSOM mechanism seems more physiologically justified.

Moreover ITSOM can also be used in a supervised fashion, as it can learn from a set of examples and use the obtained z-scores to recognized new patterns. The fact that learning can be both supervised and unsupervised seems confirmed by the everyday experience and by several studies [41][42][43][44][45][46][47][48].

C. Dynamical Analysis of ITSOM

The SOM can be expressed as a non-linear dynamical model expressed by the differential equation [49] [50]

$$\frac{dx_i}{dt} = I_i - \mu(x_i)$$

where the output variable x_i can be matched to the average firing rate of the neuron i, I_i is the combined effect of all inputs to the neuron i, and $\mu(x_i)$ the sum of all the non-linear losses of the firing process.

As mentioned above, the SOM architecture was studied by T. Kohonen following his neurophysiological studies, observing the WTA function in the cortex [51].

B. Ermentrout [52] studied a cortical model in which the WTA process has the dual role of selecting the most important stimulus and strengthening the patterns after the disappearance of the stimulus.

The author shows that every time a neuron is active for a certain time and then stops firing, the network oscillates between different states, as "ponies on a merry-go-round".

The author explains that the limit cycles that are created are the effect of the bifurcation solutions of system

$$\frac{dx_i}{dt} = -\mu x_j + F\left(x_j,\ u(t); \alpha\right) \quad j = 1,\ ...,\ N$$

for N activated neurons x_j, where $F(x,\ y;\ \alpha)$ is a function of two variables parameterized by α and such that

$$\frac{F(\cdot)}{dx} > 0 \quad \text{and} \quad \frac{F(\cdot)}{dy} < 0,$$

and *u(t)* is the inhibitory feedback of the form

$$u(t) = G\left(\sum_k x_k\right)$$

where G is monotonically increasing.

The overall activity $x_1(t) + \ldots + x_j(t)$ is shown to lie almost on a closed trajectory, that means that the total excitatory network activity remains almost constant.

Traub as well [53] presents a biophysical model of this effect in which, even if the individual neurons fire, the whole system has a regular behavior, forming "limit cycles that preserve the order."

5 EXAMPLES OF ANALYSIS OF
NON-LINEAR DYNAMICAL SYSTEMS

A. Application to the equalization and demodulation of GSM Signals

The GSM signal is a highly non-linear signal, affected by Gaussian noise, multiple reflections, fading and Doppler effect. Only thanks to sophisticated algorithms of error correction it is possible to reconstruct a satisfactory signal.

Most of the techniques incorporate equalizers and Viterbi demodulators based on the maximum likelihood principle recovering the signal adaptively.

A receiver consists of an equalizer and a demodulator in cascade. An equalizer is a tool that at the end of the transmission chain compensates for unwanted features of the channel and provides to the demodulator a sequence of symbols, to which the demodulator will have to assign the correct decision region. The structure of a standard equalizer makes use of a tapped delay line that stores n samples x_n which are linearly changed to produce the equalizer output

$$y_n = \underline{c} x_n$$

where $\underline{c}$ is the taps vector.

To properly reconstruct the x_n samples it is necessary to optimize the tap vector, and to do this a gradient algorithm is used that minimizes the error recursively, very similar to the gradient descent algorithm [81].

Demodulation is instead essentially a mapping of the signals received on an expected set of symbols. The most powerful demodulator, the Viterbi demodulator, uses a convolutional decoding method.

However the Viterbi algorithm is computationally burdensome, heavy and expensive in its hardware version, and is a substantially linear technique used on a strongly non-linear signal. Moreover also the Viterbi algorithm, as all the traditional algorithms, quickly becomes suboptimal if the characteristics of the signal deviate from their theoretical values [54].

ANNs are therefore, at least in principle, an effective alternative to the classic equalization and demodulation techniques: in fact have a natural similarity to standard equalizers and are good classifiers even on topologically complex sets, but more than standard equalizers and demodulators they can perform non-linear processing [55] [56] [57].

A neural receiver must be able to handle time-varying communication channels. Many different schemes have been proposed for space-time pattern processing. As seen in Chapter 3, the best performances are achieved with strictly dynamical networks, endowed with "state feedback" , carried out with appropriate connections between nodes: the nodes receive as input signals both the input and the output obtained from the network at the previous time.

A neural receiver (equalizer + demodulator) has been tested using QPSK modulation of a channel affected by fading and Doppler effect. Bandwidth limiting, which is a typical feature of real channels, and also causes interference inter-symbol (ISI), ie overlap of successive signals in time, was obtained with Butterworth and Chebiceff filters.

The information was encoded by a NRZ (Not Return to Zero) sequence (simulated by a sequence generator of + 1 / -1 bits) divided into packages with the structure of the GSM bursts (148 bits, of which 3 head and 3 tails, 58 bits of information, 26 known (middamble), 58 bits of information).

QPSK modulation associates with the word to be transmitted 4 symbols corresponding to the phase shifts of the transmitted carrier.

The 2 bits sequence that codes a symbol corresponds to a phase shift expressible as a phase and a quadrature value. In this way, a one to one correspondence is achieved between the bits to be recovered and the numerical value of phase and quadrature, which allows the network to obtain a one to one correspondence between the channel output and sequence of the source bits [58][59].

To test the performances of ANNs as receivers, an RBP network based on the Williams/Pineda model [60][61] (see Chapter 3) was initially used.

The number of nodes used for the RBP network was selected experimentally, getting the best performance with 74 input nodes, 74 hidden and output 148, which allow the network to maintain a symmetry around the middamble. The network was trained by providing data through a delay line whose number of taps was set equal to the number of the network input nodes. The system produces an output that is function of the current input and of the previous output.

The radiomobile channel conditions of rural, hilly and urban terrain, with speeds 10,50,100 and 250 kmh have been simulated.

The receiver was compared with the performance of coherent and Viterbi receivers, both in conditions of infinite bandwidth and using Butterworth and Chebiceff filters with different characteristics.

The described approach limits are twofold: on one hand the training time is extremely slow (more than 48 hours on a 5000/240 DECstation), on the other hand, it is impossible to obtain a weights matrix effective for any channel variation. While the training phase shows an almost perfect capacity to recover the signal, the testing phase improves with the increasing of the number of samples and shows an interesting insensitivity to the increase of SNR, but performances remain high only using different weights matrices for each terrain on which the simulations are performed. The need to create arrays of different weights for different channel conditions makes it difficult to imagine an industrial use of the network, because an algorithm should be provided that automatically detects the type of terrain and shifts to the suitable weights matrix.

An attempt to follow the channel fluctuations training a small RBP network in real time proved to be unsuccessful, because the network fails to generalize if not in presence of an adequate number of samples. For this reason, unsupervised ANNs [62][63] appear a better choice to develop a neural receiver able to adapt in real time to the channel fluctuations.

An ITSOM network with 74 input nodes and 74 recurrence nodes was implemented, with a number of competitive layer nodes between 15 and 35, used as a demodulator and equalizer in cascade. The network allows to be tuned by different parameters: a learning rate, a "forgetfulness" rate that punishes the neurons external to the neighborhood, and a conscience [64] which limits the number of winning events for each neuron, avoiding the polarization on few neurons.

The parameters on which the network was shown more sensitive were the learning rate and the competitive layer dimension.

The simulation on the individual input bits highlights chaotic, sometimes cyclical attractors, formed by periodic successions of winning neurons (Simulink, Runge-Kutta method) (Fig. 9).

The stability of the system attractors keeps with the epochs growing.

The existence of organized patterns within the time series of the winning nodes for each input element is confirmed by the autocorrelation function [65].

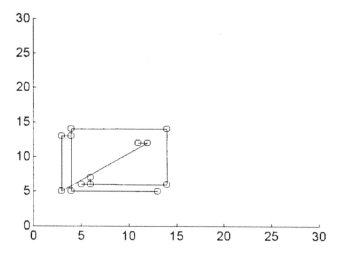

Fig. 9 - Attractor of the winning neurons for the -1 bit

For univariate series the autocorrelation function of a series of mean μ and variance σ^2 is given by

$$\gamma(k) = E(x_i - \mu)(x_{i+k} - \mu)$$

$$\rho(k) = \frac{\gamma(k)}{\sigma_x^2} \qquad k = 0 \pm 1, \pm 2, ...$$

autocovariance function of the series $x(t)$ at lag k.

The autocorrelation diagram shows the presence or the absence of temporal correlation between the terms of a series.

In this case all diagrams show sinusoidal pattern, evidence of cyclical components inside the series.

Moreover, the shape of the single bit diagrams is similar to the shape of the same value bits (Fig. 10, Fig.11), confirming the correspondence between an organized pattern created by the series of the winning neurons and a specific class of bits.

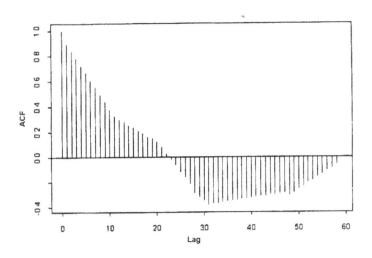

Fig. 10 - Autocorrelation function shape of the -1 bit

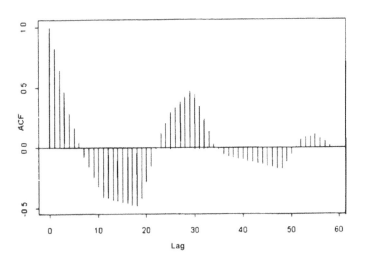

Fig. 11- Autocorrelation function shape of the +1 bit

The network performances with infinite bandwidth and filter-limited bandwidth were compared both on Gaussian channel and on channel affected by fading for rural, hilly and urban terrain.

The comparison with the Viterbi demodulator shows better performances of the ANN in the Gaussian case, while on the channel affected by fading, on any terrain, the ANN remains competitive (Fig.12).

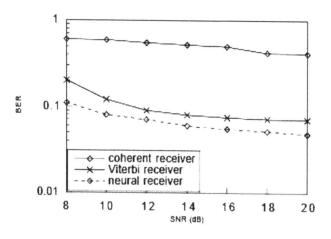

Fig.12 – Performance comparison in limited bandwidth AWGN channel

Adding Chebiceff filters the ANN performances are always comparable to those of the Viterbi receiver, even in extreme conditions (Chebiceff filter with 4 to 6 poles, bandwidth normalized from 0.9 to 0.7).

In all cases, the ANN shows better performances than both the coherent and the differential demodulator.

If we compare the ITSOM performance with the MSE standard

equalizer, we note that the ITSOM shows significantly higher performances on all conditions. We can conclude that the neural receiver shows extremely competitive performances compared to the optimal receiver.

However, while the neural receiver works in real time by tracking the non-linear channel fluctuations, the Viterbi demodulator performances presented in the graphs are always calculated on a channel whose statistics is a-priori known: in the real conditions Viterbi performances immediately become suboptimal.

Finally it should be noted that on all the conditions the ITSOM shows to perform better than the Recurrent backpropagation networks. The feasibility of an ITSOM-based neural receiver is also particularly interesting for the lower (logarithmic) computational complexity compared to the (exponential) Viterbi algorithm [66] [67] [68].

B. Non-Linear Analysis of Cortical Signals and Functional Binding of Perceptions

An application of the non-linear analysis methods has been tested in the study of the so-called binding problem, i.e. the problem of understanding the origin of the perceptual unity of consciousness in the multiplicity of sensory stimuli.

Many neurophysiologists [69][70][71][72][73][74][75][76] have proposed that such unity can be related to the self-organization of gamma waves (~ 40 Hz) emitted by the cortical neurons, which in many studies show to synchronize under sensory stimuli among distant sites, and may therefore create a functional binding.

It was proposed that the oscillation activity at high frequency in the limbic cortex may be linked to the functional binding related to high-level cognitive functions such as memory and learning.

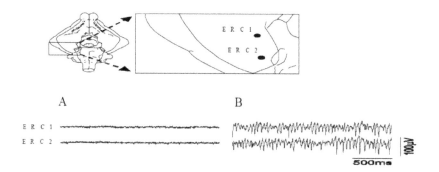

Fig. 13 - Entorhinal cortex median - signals before and after carbachol administration

Global coherent patterns of neuronal activity are considered by influent neuroscientists as the main neural correlate of conscious experience [16][17].

The ability to simultaneously record the activity of distant cortex sites through microelectrodes led to the possibility to analyze the mechanism by which the activity of a collection of neurons can be coordinated in a unique pattern.

It was proposed that neurons in the sensory cortex interact extensively and that the action potentials evoked by stimuli lead to the emergence of a self-organized pattern of activity as a cortical response to the stimulus [69].

In order to evaluate the possible correlations in the neural signals the above described ITSOM network model was used, to highlight the presence of limit cycles or chaotic attractors.

Non-linear analysis tools were also used to assess quantitatively the attractors generated by the network, namely: correlation dimension, Hurst parameter and Recurrence Quantification Analysis.

The same parameters were used to analyze the original time series, and the results were compared from both sources.

Electrophysiological signals were obtained from the brains of guinea pig isolated artificially [70]. It was seen that the gamma activity can be induced in the median entorhinal cortex (ERC) of guinea pigs which is administered carbachol (50-100 mM), simulating the attentional activity in the presence of a sensory stimulus.

The gamma activity is recorded simultaneously at different points (up to 20) separated by about 1 mm in the median ERC [71].

Several files derived from 4 different monitoring sites in the entorhinal cortex were recorded before, during and after the simulation of an attentional stimulation by administration of carbachol (Fig. 13).

The signals were considered simultaneously on all recording sites to assess their correlation. The same records were used as input for the ITSOM network, and the time series of the winning neurons was processed with a MATLAB (MATLAB and Simulink 2012b, The MathWorks, Inc., Natick, MA, USA) procedure. The procedure allowed to highlight the presence of limit cycles or chaotic attractors, displaying their trajectory in the phase space.

Under control conditions (before the activation of the fast oscillations), the graphs show some organization on the single record, but patterns with random structure or poorly organized appear in case of signals processed simultaneously from multiple sites.

However, after the induction of oscillatory activity through the application of carbachol, more chaotic patterns appear, with similar but never identical values, and strongly symmetrical shapes (Fig. 14).

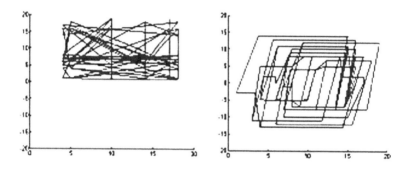

Fig. 14 - Weight space attractors before and after carbachol administration

In order to quantitatively evaluate the attractors, Hurst parameter, correlation dimension and Recurrence Quantitative Analysis [72] have been used.

The Hurst parameter, constantly under the value of 0.4 before carbachol, grows sharply after carbachol and exceeded the threshold of 0.5, often reaching 0.8. This indicates that the signals become organized during the stimulus and keep the organization for a time after the stimulus.

The correlation dimension does not appear to be a significant parameter because it keeps constant in the range 2.6-3.2 (using 10 as the embedding dimension value) before and after the stimulus: this value seems to be a feature of the type of signal.

It should be noted that the size> 2 shows a generic chaotic behavior of the series.

On the other hand the measurement of determinism of the embedded series, evaluated with the Recurrent Quantification Analysis (RQA), confirms the same increase after the stimulus shown by the Hurst parameter, jumping up to over 90% and keeping this very high value for a time.

The Recurrence Plots confirm the existence of extremely regular and evocative patterns in correspondence to high values of H (Fig. 15 and 16).

The contextual analysis of the original time series with linear methods (coherence computed through power spectrum and cross power spectrum) tested on distant sites confirms an increase in values after the stimulus but is maintained lower than 0.4 in all tests. The non-linear analysis on the single record or two records essentially confirms the ITSOM results.

In some cases sharp differences of the parameter values are have been detected whose neurophysiological meaning is not known and should be investigated more closely.

In general, we can conclude that the ITSOM network identifies self-organizing structures more often than linear numerical analysis. This may suggest a finer sensitivity of ANNs, although the possibility of false positives cannot be ruled out.

On the other hand, the values of the Hurst parameter derived from the ITSOM are often higher than the corresponding values derived from the original series.

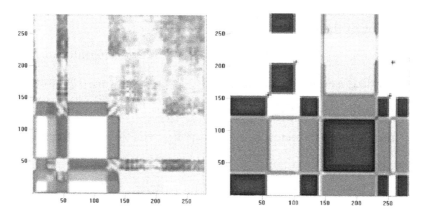

Fig.15 - Recurrence plots of the series of the winning neurons

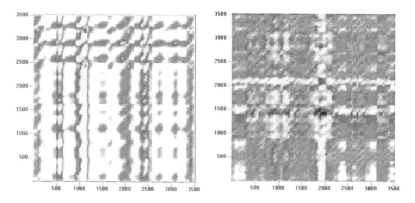

Fig. 16 - Recurrence Plots of the original series

It should also be pointed out that, unlike non-linear analysis on the original series, the analysis carried out with the ANN made it possible to simultaneously analyze all the recording sites, testing their possible synchronicity.

It is also possible, once an organized pattern is found, to identify it by its z-score and to recognize the same attractor every time the set of signals generates one.

In conclusion, the existence of a non-linear coherence (in the form of chaotic attractors) in rapid oscillations induced on guinea pig cortex is confirmed, suggesting a possible functional binding of chaotic nature between distant regions of the entorhinal cortex.

The ITSOM method can test the coherence of records simultaneously from all sites. It is also possible to deepen the analysis of the meaning of these patterns through the possibility to compare similar attractors in time.

W. Freeman researches ([15] and subsequent work) have proposed, through a study with microelectrodes implanted on the cortex of rabbits and recorded during the experimental release of smells, that cortical neurons interact extensively highlighting chaotic spatiotemporal patterns, repetitive in correspondence of a specific smell and different in response to different stimuli.

The ITSOM ANN non-linear analysis confirms the hypothesis that the coordinated 40 Hz activity of cortical neurons may clarify the origin of the sensory "binding" that we all perceive.

REFERENCES

[1] F. Heylighen, "Self-Organization, Emergence and the Architecture of Complexity" Proc. European Congress on System Science, AFCET Paris, pp. 23-32, 1992.

[2] M. Gell-Mann, " What is Complexity ?" Complexity 1, pp. 16-19, 1995.

[3] R.K. Standisch, "On complexity and emergence" Complexity Int., vol. 9, 2002 .

[4] R. Rosen, Foundations of Mathematical Biology, Ac. Press New York, 1972.

[5] E.N. Lorenz, " Deterministic Nonperiodic Flow" J. Atmos. Sci., Vols. 20, , no. 130, 1963.

[6] J. Gleick, " Chaos," Viking New York, 1987.

[7] D. Green, "Emergent behavior in biological systems", Complexity Int., vol. 1, April 1994.

[8] D. Kaplan, L. Glass, Understanding Nonlinear Dynamics, Springer, 1995.

[9] E. Jackson, Perspectives in Nonlinear Dynamics, Cambridge Un. Press , vol. 1&2, 1989.

[10] H. Atmanspacher, J. Kurths, "Complexity and Meaning in

Nonlinear Dynamical Systems," Open Systems and Information Dynamics, vol. 1, pp. 269-289, 1992.

[11] R. Rosen, "Dynamical System Theory in Biology," in: Stability Theory and its applications, vol. 1, Wiley Interscience Series on Biomedical Engineering., 1970.

[12] H.O. Peitgen, H.Jurgens, D.Saupe, Chaos and Fractals. New Frontiers of Science, Springer , 1992.

[13] B. Mandelbrot, The Fractal Geometry of Nature, Freedman & Co, 1983.

[14] E. Ott, "Appendix: Hausdorff Dimension", in: Chaos in Dynamical Systems, New York, Cambridge University Press, pp. 100-103, 1993.

[15] W.J. Freeman, "Relation of olfactory EEG on behaviour: time series analysis," Behavioural Neuroscience , vol. 100, 1987.

[16] W.J. Freeman, "Role of Chaotic Dynamics in Neural Plasticity, in: The Self-organizing Brain: from Growth Cones to Functional Networks, J.Van Pelt. da F. Silva. (eds) Elsevier, 1994.

[17] V. Menon, W.J. Freeman, "Spatio-temporal Correlations in Human Gamma Band Electrocorticograms," Electroenc. and Clin. Neurophys, no. 98, pp. 89-102, 1996.

[18] H.E. Schepers, J.Van Beek, B. J. Bassingthwaighte, "Four methods to estimate the fractal dimension from self-affine signal," IEEE Engineering in Medicine and Biology , vol. 11, pp. 57-64, 1992.

[19] P. Grassberger, I. Procaccia, "Measuring the strangeness of a strange attractor," Physica D, vol. 9, pp. 189-208, 1983.

[20] H.E. Hurst, R.P. Black, Y. M. Sinai, "Long Term Storage in reservoirs. An Experimental Study," Constable , 1965.

[21] J.P. Zbilut, C.L. Webber, "Embeddings and delays as derived from quantification of Recurrent plot", Phys Lett. 171, 1992.

[22] C. Jeffries, Code Recognition and Set Selection with Neural Network, Birkhauser Boston, 1991..

[23] R. Hecht-Nielsen, Neurocomputing, Addison Wesley, 1 990.

[24] J.J. Hopfield, "Neural Networks and Physical Systems with Emergent Collective Computational Abilities," Proc. Nat. Acad. Sci USA, no. 81, 1984.

[25] D. Rumelhart, J. McClelland, Parallel Distributed Processing: Explorations in microstructure of Cognition, MIT Press, 1986.

[26] A. Maren, D. Jones, "Neural Networks for Spatio-temporal Pattern Recognition," in: Handbook of Neural Computation Applications, Maren A.J., Harston C.T., Pap R.M. eds, Academic Press , 1991.

[27] A. Maren, D. Jones, "Configuring and Optimizing the Back-Propagation Network," in: Handbook of Neural Computing Applications, Maren A.J., Harston C.T., Pap R.M., Academic Press, 1991.

[28] Y. Bengio, P. Frasconi, M. Gori., G. Soda, "Recurrent Neural Networks for Adaptive Temporal Processing," Proc. Neural Nets WIRN Vietri 1993, Salerno , 1993.

[29] F.J. Pineda, "Generalization of Backpropagation to Recurrent and Higher order Neural Networks," Physical Review Letters," no. 18, pp. 2229-2232, 1987.

[30] T.A. Catfolis, "Method for improving the real-time Recurrent learning algorithm," Neural Networks, vol. 6, pp. 807-821, 1993.

[31] K. Funahashi, Y. Nakamura, "Approximation of Dynamical Systems by Continuous Time Recurrent Neural Networks," Neural Networks, vol. 6, 1993.

[32] S. Sudharsanan, M.S Sudharsanan, "Equilibrium Characterization of Dynamical Neural Networks and a Systematic Synthesis Procedure for Associative Memories," IEEE Trans. on Neural Networks, vol. 7, no. 5, Sept. 1991 .

[33] K.S. Narendra, K. Parthasarathy, "Gradient methods for the optimization of dynamical systems using neural networks," IEEE Trans. on Neural Networks, no. 2, pp. 252-262, March 1991.

[34] R.J. Williams, D. Zipser, "A learning algorithm for continually running fully Recurrent neural network," Neural Computation, pp. 270-280, 1989.

[35] R.J. Williams, J.Peng, "An efficient gradient-based algorithm for on-line training of Recurrent network trajectories.," Neural Comp , vol. 2, no. 4, pp. 490-501 , 1990.

[36] S. Grossberg, "Recent Developments in the Design of real-time non-linear Neural Networks Architectures," IEEE First Int. Conf on Neural Networks, San Diego,1987.

[37] S. Grossberg, G.A. Carpenter, "Self-organization Neural Network Architectures for Real-Time Adaptive Pattem Recognition," in: Zometzer S.F. ed., An Introduction to Neural and Electronic Networks, Academic Press, 1990.

[38] G.A. Carpenter, S. Grossberg, J.H.Reynolds, "ARTMAP: Supervised real-time learning and classification of nonstationary data by a self-organizing neural network," Neural Networks, vol. 4, no. 5, p. 565, 199 1 .

[39] M.A. Cohen, S. Grossberg, D. Stork " Recent Developments in a Neural Model of Real-Time Speech Analysis and Synthesis," IEEE First International Conf on Neural Networks, vol. 4, 1987.

[40] T. Kohonen, Self-Organisation and Association Memory, Springer Verlag, 1983.

[41] J. E. Ormrod, Human Learning, 3rd edition, Upper Saddle River, Prentice-Hall, NJ, 1999.

[42] J. Gruart, R. Leal-Campanario, J.C. Lòpez-Ramos, M. J. Delgado-Garcìa, "Functional basis of associative learning and its relationships with long-term potentiation evoked in the involved neural circuits: Lessons from studies in behaving mammals.," Neurobiology of Learning and Memory Elsevier, no. 124, pp. 3-18, 2015.

[43] A.J. Tierney, "The evolution of learned and innate behavior: Contributions from genetics and neurobiology to a theory of behavioral evolution," Animal Learning and Behavior, vol. 14, no. 4, p. 339–348, 1986.

[44] R.P. Keeling, J. Stevens Dickson, T. Avery, "Biological Bases for Learning and Development Across the Lifespan," In London M. (ed.) The Oxford Handbook of Lifelong Learning, New York: Oxford University Press, pp. 40-51, 2011.

[45] J. Willis, "Current Impact of Neuroscience on Teaching and Learning," Mind, Brain, Education: Neuroscience Implications for the Classroom, pp. 45-66, 2010.

[46] S.L. Willis, K.W. Schaie, M. Martin, "Cognitive Plasticity", in Bengtson Handbook of Theories of Aging, New York: Springer, 2009.

[47] R. Pizzi, D. Rossetti, G. Cino , D. Marino, A. Vescovi "Learning in human neural networks on microelectrode arrays," Biosystems, vol. 88, pp. 1-15, 2007.

[48] R. Pizzi, D. Rossetti, G. Cino, D. Marino, A.Vescovi, W. Bear, "A cultured human neural network operates a robotic actuator.," Biosystems, vol. 95, pp. 137-144, 2009.

[49] H. Ritter, K.Schulten "On the Stationary State of Kohonen's Self-Organizing Sensory Mapping," Biological Cybernetics, no. 54., pp. 99-106, 1986.

[50] H. Ritter, K.Schulten "Convergence properties of Kohonen's Topology Conserving Maps: Fluctuations, Stability, and Dimension Selection," Biological Cybernetics , no. 60, pp. 59-71, 1988.

[51] T. Kohonen, "Physiological Interpretation of the Self-Organizing Map Algorithm," Neural Networks, vol. 6, pp. 895-905, 1993.

[52] B. Ermentrout, "Complex Dynamics in WTA Neural Networks with slow inhibition," Neural Networks , vol. 5, 1992.

[53] R. Traub, R. Miles, Neuronal Networks of the Hippocampus, Cambridge Un. Press, 1991.

[54] J.G. Proakis, Digital Communications, McGraw-Hill, 1983.

[55] T. Petsche, B.W. Dickinson " Trellis Codes Receptive Fields and Fault Tolerant, Self- Repairing Neural Networks," IEEE Trans. on Neural Networks, vol. 1, no. 2, June 1990.

[56] G. Pfeiffer, "Maximum Likelihood Sequence Estimation of Minimum Shift Keying Signals Using a Hopfield Neural Network," in International Joint Conference on Neural Networks, S. Francisco, 1993.

[57] C. Pham, T. Ogunfunmi, "Multiple-Symbol Diffrential Detection of M-DPSK Using Neural Network," in IEEE Intemational Conference on Neural Networks, Orlando , 1994.

[58] W. Xiao-An, S.B. Wickers "An Artificial Neural Net Viterbi Decoder," IEEE Trans. On Comm., vol. 44, no. 2, Feb 1996.

[59] L.Favalli, R.Pizzi, A. Mecocci, "Non linear Mobile Radio Channel Estimation Using Neural Networks," in Proc. of DSP97 Int. Conf. on Digital Signal Processing, Crete, 1997).

[60] J.W. Watterson, "An Optimum Multilayer Perceptron Neural Receiver for Signal Detection," IEEE Trans. on Neural Networks, vol. 1, no. 4, December 1990.

[61] G. Kechriotis, E. Zervas, E.S. Manolakos, "Using Recurrent Neural Networks for Adaptive Communication Channel Equalization," IEEE Trans. on Neural Network, vol. 5, no. 2, March 1994.

[62] T. Kohonen, "Combining Linear Equalization and Self-Organizing Adaptation in Dynamic Discrete-Signal Detection," in International Joint Conference on Neural Networks, San

Diego, 1990.

[63] H. Ritter, K. Obermayer, K. Schulten, J. Rubner, Self-Organizing Maps and Adaptive Filters Models of Neural Network, E. Domany, Springer , 1993.

[64] D. Desieno, " Adding Conscience to competitive learning," Proc. Int. Conf. On Neural Networks IEEE Press , vol. 1, 1988.

[65] P.J. Brockwell, R.A. Davis, "Time Series: Theory and Methods," Springer Series in Statistics, 1991.

[66] J. Choi, S.H. Bang, B.J. Sheu, "A Programmable Analog VLSI Neural Network Processor for Communication receivers," IEEE Trans on Neural Networks, vol. 4, no. 3, 1993.

[67] O. Chen, B. Sheu, W. Fang "Image Compression on VLSI Neural-based Vector Quantizer," Information Processing and Management, vol. 28, no. 6, 1992..

[68] R. Pizzi, "Teoria dei Sistemi Dynamici Neurali con Applicazione alle Telecomunicazioni ", PhD Thesis, Electronic Engineering, University of Pavia, 1997.

[69] S. Amari, "Dynamical stability of Formation of Cortical Maps,," Dynamic Interaction in Neural Networks: Models and Data, 1988.

[70] C.T. Dickson, G. Biella , M. de Curtis, "Evidence for spatial modules mediated by temporal synchronization of carbachol-induced gamma rhythm in medial entorhinal cortex," J Neurosc, no. 20 , pp. 7846-7854, 2000.

[71] J.J. Chrobak, G. Buzsaki,"Gamma oscillations in the entorhinal cortex of the freely behaving rat.," J Neurosci , pp. 388-398,

1998.

[72] R. Pizzi, de M. Curtis, C. Dickson, "Evidence of Chaotic Attractors in Cortical Fast Oscillations Tested by an Artificial Neural Network," in: Advances in Soft Computing, pp. 11-22, Springer Physica-Verlag, 2003.

[73] M. Joliot, U. Ribary, R. Llinas, "Human oscillatory brain activity near 40 Hz coexists with cognitive temporal binding,," Proc. Natl. Acad. Sci USA 91 , pp. 11748-11751, 1994.

[74] W.H.R. Mitner, C. Braun, M. Arnold, H. Witten, E. Taub, "Coherence of Gammaband EEG Activity as a Basis for Associative Learning," Nature, no. 397 , pp. 434-436, 1999.

[75] E. Rodriguez, N. George, P. J. Lachaux, J. Martinerie, B. Renault and F.J. Varela, "Perception's Shadow: Long-distance Synchronization of Human Brain Activity," Nature, no. 397, pp. 430-433, 1999.

[76] F.J. Varela, "Resonant cell assemblies: a new approach to cognitive function and neuronal synchrony," Biol. Res. vol. 28, pp. 81-95 , 1995.

The Authors

RITA PIZZI is Senior Researcher at the Department of Computer Science of the University of Milan. She had her MS in Physics and her PhD in Electronic Engineering. Her main interests involve computational intelligence methods and their applications to the biomedical field. In 2009 she developed a bionic creature connecting a network of human neural stem cells to a robot with a bidirectional ANN-driven interface. Currently she is developing a computational intelligence method to codify neural correlates of qualia. More details on her research activity and the list of publications can be found at the page http://www.di.unimi.it/pizzi .

MARIALESSIA MUSUMECI had her BS in Neurophysiology Techniques and her MS in Cognitive Science and Decision Making at the University of Milan. Then she continued her professional experience at the Advanced Biotechnology Center, consortium of the Ministry of Research. She is currently PhD student at the Department of Computer Science of the University of Milan.

www.ingramcontent.com/pod-product-compliance
Lightning Source LLC
Chambersburg PA
CBHW052150070326
40690CB00048B/2559